How to Make Money Blogging:
How I Replaced My Day Job With My Blog

Bob Lotich

ISBN-13: 978-0-9898945-0-0

Table of Contents

Note from the Author

The purpose of this book is to show you how to make money with a blog. I suspect most people won't stick with it long enough to make a full-time income, but even making an extra few hundred dollars a month isn't too bad either.

This book is fairly short. I am a very to-the-point type of guy, and I much prefer the meat and potatoes over a bunch of fluff. So, rather than fill this book with fluff, I'm keeping it very concise and full of helpful information for new to intermediate bloggers.

If you're around the blogging world, even a bit, you'll quickly realize there are a lot of bloggers who make money by talking about how to make money online. Rather than just talking about it, I chose to see if I could actually make a full-time living before ever wrote about it at all.

That's not to say there isn't plenty to learn from unproven bloggers, but I felt more comfortable proving to myself I could do it before teaching others. Now that I've found it's actually a legit way to earn some money, I decided to pour into this book as much as I could about blogging.

If you find the book helpful, or if you see ways I can improve the book, or even if you hate it and want a refund, please let me know. I greatly appreciate your feedback, and it will help me continue to tweak and improve the book – so thank you in advance!

If you enjoy this book, for a limited time I am hosting a free 60-minute online workshop where I share the 3 biggest secrets that helped me turn my blog into a full-time living.

I will only be hosting these workshops for a limited time, so if you are interested be sure to pop over to get registered.

Just visit EfficientBlogging.com/join to get registered for free.

Sincerely,
Bob Lotich

1. How it all started for me

In early 2007 I was talking to a friend of mine about the idea of building websites full of free information to help people. After brainstorming a bit, I got a couple of ideas for topics I'm passionate about: Proverbs and personal finance.

My first idea was to post a Proverb each day and comment on it. As I explained my idea further to my friend, he told me I would basically have a blog. I didn't know what a blog was, but I thought, "Oh, OK, sure."

So, over the next few weeks I read as much as I could find about blogging and ultimately decided to create a blog about personal finance from a Christian perspective. I'm very interested in helping people with their money, so blogging seemed like a great way to reach people all over the world.

Over the next couple months I started writing articles and officially launched SeedTime.com (formerly ChristianPF.com) in June 2007. At this point I thought about making money from the site but had no idea how and honestly didn't really think it was possible to make a living at it. I put up an Adsense ad just to see what would happen, and I still remember how excited I was when I saw that I made my first seven cents!

From there, I set a goal to make $100 by the end of 2007, which was fairly easy to accomplish – even without knowing anything.

I should also mention that from June 2007 to June 2008 I spent about four to six hours each weekend writing articles and averaged about four new articles each week. Also, I spent a few more hours during the week on site maintenance, emails, social media, etc. So in total I probably spent about 10 hours each week working on the site.

Getting laid off

In July 2008 things got interesting; a larger firm bought out the large brokerage firm where I worked for five years. I was told the company no longer needed my department, so they handed me a severance check, and I was on my way. I was making some money from the blog but not enough to even pay the rent each month.

After much prayer and discussion with my wife I decided against looking for another "day job" and to work full time on building the blog. We had paid off most of our debt and had my wife's income as a support to buy us some time. I figured I'd give it a shot for a few months, and if it didn't work out, I'd find another 9-5. From that point the income generated from my blog increased each month and in February 2009 – for the first time – it exceeded my monthly income from my old day job.

I'm still a little bit in awe and can't believe I'm actually paying the bills from my blog! But I thank God every day that I get to do what I love and get paid to do it. I really did not enjoy the corporate America thing and am so thankful to do what I do! It's hard work, but it doesn't really seem like it when you're doing something you're passionate about and love doing.

Regardless of what your personal long-term blogging goals are, keep on reading, and I'll try to help you take the next steps towards reaching them!

2. Four steps to get started blogging in 10 minutes!

First things first, if you haven't started your blog yet, head over to this link and get my free 14-Point Blog Startup Checklist here:

http://EfficientBlogging.com/startup

Trust me, you will be glad you did.

And you can follow these steps below, but this is just a quick Cliffs Notes version. (For more detail finish reading the book!) These recommendations are the things I would do if I had to do it all over again today.

1. Find a domain name

- Go to Domize.com and find a domain name that's available (blue ones are open, red ones are taken, and green ones are pricey) but don't purchase it yet.
- If possible, aim for a domain name that has at least some of the keywords you want people to find in the search engines.

2. Get a domain name and web hosting package

- There are thousands of webhosts out there, but Hostgator.com is my favorite for reasons we'll cover later. Head over to Hostgator.com and select either the "Hatchling" or "Baby" plan.
- Then make sure you register the domain you found in the first step.
- Next enter "EFFICIENT30" as a promo code and it will knock 30 percent off for you.

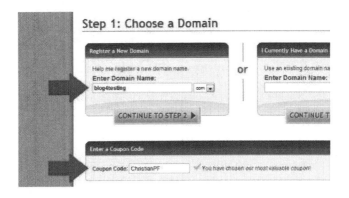

- Now follow the remaining steps to complete your purchase.

3. Install WordPress (with a little help)

- Jump on the phone or use the chat box with Hostgator.
- When you get someone on the line, just say you want to install WordPress on your blog.
- Whoever you're talking to will hold your hand and walk you through the process (if not, please email me). When complete ask for the WordPress login information.

4. Login to WordPress

- Once you have the login information, you can go to http://www.yourdomain.com/wp-admin and login.
- Now that you're logged in to WordPress, you can begin making changes to your site and/or publish your first post.

If you need more detailed instructions I am happy to offer you FREE access to my step-by-step video course as a thank you bonus for picking up this book.

The course will walk you through every single detail of setting up your WordPress blog and a whole lot more!

You can get your bonus here: EfficientBlogging.com/bonus.

3. Blogging basics

I'll try to boil this down to the essentials. There are whole books written on this subject, so I won't to try to cover everything here. But for a quick, bottom-line version keep reading.

What is a blog?

A blog is short for Web log. Basically, it's just a website that has entries listed in reverse chronological order. The original idea behind it was to be an online journal or diary that was updated daily (or as frequently as the writer chose).

During the past decade many software companies have created programs and blogging platforms to make the process VERY EASY. As the blog writer, depending on which platform you use, you can just type your entry, press submit, and it shows up on your blog for the world to see. Most bloggers don't know any programming languages and are not "techies," and these companies know that.

Starting a blog is one of the easiest ways out there to start a website. If you haven't started one yet, why not try it? It can be very quick to set up and is sometimes completely free.

Is it easy to start a blog?

It's very easy. Even if there are steps along the way that are confusing, there are plenty of resources to get the help you need. There are more than 20 million blogs in existence, so starting a blog can't be that difficult.

How much does it cost to blog?

There are many services that allow you to start a blog for free. If you're just trying out this whole blogging thing, try using one of the free services to get a basic feel for blogging and get your feet wet.

Once you decide you want to stick with it and that you want to make money with your blog, you may want to move up to a self-hosted blog. Anyone who is really trying to make money with a blog will probably find more success with a self-hosted blog. Getting a self-hosted blog probably isn't free but still can be VERY inexpensive. You need to pay for nothing more than a domain name (about $10/yr) and webhosting (as cheap as a few bucks a month).

Getting a blogging platform

All three of the options listed below are free. The first two options are the easiest but are also limited on features. If you are just trying to make an extra few hundred dollars from your blog, these options could work. But if you're really serious about trying to make good money from your blog, try self-hosting your blog (which we talk about in the next section).

Blogger.com – Blogger is very good and easy to set up, and Google owns it. You can customize the theme, and the domain name includes ".blogspot.com." (In some people's opinion this is a little less professional.) Blogger continues to become more customizable and currently has a lot more options than it did a few years ago.

WordPress.com – These sites are completely free and easy to set up, and you can customize the theme, but other customizations are limited, domain name includes ".wordpress.com." The big downside with these sites is that they don't allow you to place ads on your blog.

WordPress.org – Wait, what's the difference between wordpress.com and wordpress.org? To put it simply, WordPress.com is where you go to set up a basic, easy blog with limited features. WordPress.org is where you go to get a self-hosted blog. If you get to the point where you're serious about blogging and really want to make some money with it, you need to self-host your blog.

4. How to set up a self-hosted blog

If you plan to use one of the first two free options from the previous section, you can skip this section.

If you're serious about blogging and looking for the best way to customize your blog's look and other features, then getting a self-hosted blog from WordPress.org is the best way to go. It's far and away the top choice for most bloggers. It does require a little more work up front and does have small costs associated with it: buying a domain name (about $10/year) and hosting your blog (< $10/month).

One of the big advantages is that you can use your own domain name (i.e., yourblog.com). While this might not seem like a big deal, it's a lot easier for people to remember yourblog.com rather than yourblog.blogspot.com, which is what you get if you use Blogger.

While it's a little more work on the front end, I'm really glad I got good advice and did this at the beginning, rather than doing it a year or two down the road.

Pick a domain name

You should start by purchasing a domain name. Domize.com is a great tool to help you find available domain names. Try going for a .com rather than a .info or .us or anything else for that matter. It's just too easy for people to get confused. A .com is always going to hold more value than any other extension.

Once you choose it, you need to find somewhere to purchase it. I bought my first few domains at GoDaddy.com and have bought the remaining ones from my hosting companies. While GoDaddy is about one of the biggest names out there, I (and many of my peers) have had bad experiences with them; so I wouldn't recommend using them. Also, it's often easier just to buy the domain from the hosting company you sign up with since it will almost always simplify the process.

Pick a host for your blog

The webhost is the company you pay to store all of your blog files. There are also a million webhosting companies out there. Don't just look for the cheapest one because a lot of these companies are not very reliable, and your site might be down quite a bit. Try going with a bigger company that has a longer track record and is more established.

They may cost a dollar or two more a month when you're starting out, but it's well worth it. I have hosted my websites with Dreamhost from the beginning, mostly because I knew a lot of people using them, and I got a hosting package for about $7 a month.

Now, I wholeheartedly recommend Hostgator.com over Dreamhost. The biggest reason is because Hostgator has staff available via phone or chat 24 hours a day. This is NOT very common for the cheaper webhosting companies. You will inevitably run into a problem with your site at some point, and it will comfort you to know you have someone to call when problems arise.

Hosting companies I've used

HostGator.com (As low as $3.96/m)

I started hosting with Hostgator after becoming increasingly frustrated with MediaTemple. From my experience Hostgator's customer service seems to surpass any other host I've used. I'm so impressed with its customer service that I now host all my sites through Hostgator (except my biggest one).

Bluehost.com (As low as $6.95/m)

I hosted a few of my sites with Bluehost, and I had a really good experience. It's cheap and has a great phone support. The only downside is that there's one hosting package, which is fine for small to medium sites but not so good if your blog continues to grow into a large blog.

Dreamhost.com (As low as $8.95/m)

As I mentioned earlier, I started with Dreamhost and was happy with it for the price, but I always longed for phone support, and the company doesn't really offer it. If you decide to use it, I have a coupon code you can use for 25 percent off. Just enter "Christianblog" as the promo code.

MediaTemple.net (As low as $20/m)

I hosted my main site (SeedTime.com) with MediaTemple for a couple of years, but after many bad experiences with the customer support team and frequent hold times of 45+ minutes, I left. I don't recommend them.

WPengine.com (As low as $29/m)

I now host my main site with WP Engine. The main reason I moved to WP Engine is because the whole operation is specifically for WordPress sites, and as a result, it can tweak the servers to increase site speed and minimize downtime. Also, all of the support staff is very well trained in WordPress, which is rarely the case at other hosts.

Summing it all up

HostGator is an excellent choice for new bloggers because there's dependable support, and it's cost effective. And for bloggers who want a rock-solid hosting company and can afford a little more, try WP Engine.

5. Get a customizable theme

After I took the step to self-host my blog, the next step that greatly helped me increase earnings was to choose a highly customizable theme. This costs anywhere from $50-$100 so you may not want to do it at the beginning, but once you're committed to blogging and want to invest a few bucks, putting that money toward a premium theme is a good investment.

For all my blogs I use either the Thesis theme or the Genesis theme. Without getting into all the details, if you asked me right now what the best WordPress theme was, I'd say the Genesis theme. Thesis is really good, but it has gotten more and more complex in recent months, so I normally just recommend the Genesis theme for most bloggers.

Right out of the box, it provides you with a very pretty site that's very easy to customize. It is SEO optimized very well, has a lot of bells and whistles and a ton of support. The kicker is that you can buy it and get lifetime updates for $59.

If you're a programmer, you really don't need to buy a theme because you can make all the customizations yourself to any basic theme. Since starting to blog a couple of years ago, I have learned a little HTML, but I'm still about the furthest thing from a programmer! So, for people like me, a customizable theme allows me to control things and areas on the site I could never change without the help of a programmer.

But even still, if you have a specific vision of what you want your blog to look like and aren't willing to compromise on that, you will probably need the help of a programmer/designer to help you. Elance.com is a great place to find one.

6. How I make money with my blog

When I go to family functions or social events, I often get a blank stare when I explain what I do for a living. I think people understand the part that I write articles and put them on a website, but when it comes to making money from it, they don't get it. In this section I will lay it out, and I hope it will help bring some clarity.

CPC ad networks (cost per click)

There are a few different ad networks I use on my blogs. The most successful one is Google's Adsense program. It is a cost-per-click model, which means that I get paid every time a visitor clicks one of those ads. Google's responsibility is to read the article I write and find ads that are relevant and display them next to the article. It actually is a pretty good system, and as a result it tends to be the easiest and quickest way that most bloggers start making money. Also, many of the extremely relevant ads that Adsense provides can be quite beneficial and helpful to the readers.

For example, if I write an article explaining what an IRA is, but don't mention where you can open one, Adsense will likely display ads for places to open an IRA. So, if I read that article and decided I did want to open an IRA, the ads provide options the article did not. All things considered, when Adsense ads are optimized correctly they can be a great way to earn from your blog. I'll explain more about how to optimize the ads in the following sections.

CPM ad networks

While Adsense pays on a click basis (CPC), I use other ad networks that pay by the total number of visitor impressions (CPM, cost per thousand). At the beginning these networks don't produce much income, but as the traffic grows, CPM networks seem to work well in conjunction with Adsense. I use (or have used):

- Pulsepoint.com
- AdClickMedia.com
- Adbrite.com
- Adify.com
- Technoratimedia.com
- Casalemedia.com

Each has its own strengths and weaknesses and may be suitable for one kind of a site and not another.

Affiliate product sales

Let's say you sell lawn mowers, and I refer someone to your store who's interested in buying a mower. If the customer then purchases the mower, you send me a check paying me a percent of the sales price.

This is essentially what an affiliate sale is. It isn't much different from being a 100 percent commissioned salesperson for a company except that online you can do it for multiple companies.

There are a million options to get started with affiliate ads on the Internet now. Some programs you can use are:

- Affiliate-program.amazon.com
- FlexOffers.com
- CJ.com
- Shareasale.com
- E-Junkie.com
- LinkShare.com

There are many others, but these are a few of the more popular ones available.

I have a very strong policy about honest recommendations. I give my honest opinions about products regardless of how it affects affiliate sales. For example, I wrote about Cash Crate and updated the article to show what I didn't like about it. Because Cash Crate has such a generous referral program, I know some people make lots of money from it, but I just don't feel comfortable recommending it since I had a bad experience using it.

On the other hand there are products like Ebates, YNAB, Swagbucks and Sharebuilder I recommend and also have some sort of affiliate or referral program as well. These are what I love because I can help readers by pointing them to good resources and tools that helped me and get paid in the process. I know some people don't have a problem promoting anything that will pay them, but I just can't, in good conscience, recommend something to someone that I don't genuinely believe will help them.

Direct ad sales

I also sell ad space directly to advertisers. This hasn't provided much income for me yet and may or may not even be worth my time. I know that in certain niche markets direct ad sales can work out very well, but thus far it hasn't been a big money maker on my blogs. But if you're interested in this, check out buysellads.com. The site is basically like a middleman helping bloggers and advertisers get connected.

7. How long does it take to make money from a blog?

The second question that people normally ask after, "How do I make money with a blog?" is, "How long is it going to take?" Well, let me just say this, if you're looking for a fast way to make money, blogging isn't it. It takes time and hard work. As you can see from the chart below it took me a long time before the trend started moving upward.

But for more than a year I worked at it about 10 hours a week. And don't forget I didn't know anything about blogging, advertising, getting traffic, etc. when I started. So, if you know what a blog is, then you have a head start on me. I'm going explain most of the things I didn't know the first year that I did to help create that upward trend in the following chart.

Blog earnings visualized

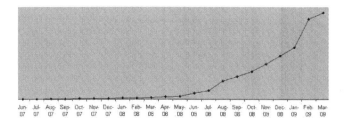

Other people I know who make a decent amount from their blogs confirm this curve is typical. While the first year didn't yield much income, it was crucial for the second year. I wish I could tell you that you could jump right ahead to where the income starts increasing more quickly, but I just don't think it's likely.

There are some tips in this book I wish I knew at the beginning, and I think they'll make things go a lot more quickly for you, but there's no getting around it's going to take time to get there. However, just like anything, the more you put in the more you get out.

The two keys are consistency and a willingness to learn.

Without them, it's very difficult to earn much money with your blog.

8. How to get traffic to your blog

If you're like most, you want to create a blog so that others can read what you have to say. Sadly, people will not find your blog (in the beginning anyway) unless you do a little legwork. These are some of the things I did to get traffic and some that I still do. The first thing to do is write a few great articles about your topic and feature them in your sidebar. Then, start working on generating traffic, because you not only want traffic, but you want returning traffic as well.

Blog commenting

One of the absolute best ways for new blogs to get traffic is just to comment on other blogs. Commenting with a thoughtful and/or provocative response will often send a few visitors your way. The blogging community is generally very social, and those who are active often reap the rewards. Even more important than the few visitors you pick up from it is the relationships you can develop with other bloggers.

Guest posting

I think this is one of the best ways to start getting some traffic and building an audience. Guest posting provides a great opportunity for a newbie to write an article that 20,000 readers can see. I don't know of any other method that could bring traffic as quickly.

The key is to write a great article – don't hold back your best stuff. I've seen people grow their blogs very quickly by posting some of their best articles on other sites. Also, only submit unpublished content as a guest post. If it's already published, then the blog that's allowing you to guest post won't get any search engine traffic for that article. There are, though, places to republish your articles. We'll get to that in a minute.

First, do a lot of commenting on some small to medium-sized blogs in your niche. Get to know the bloggers, connect with them via email or other social media, and get to know them. THEN, offer to write them a guest post.

Join directories

If I were starting a blog today, one of the first things I would do is Google "whatever topic I want to blog about" + "directory" This should return a list of web directories about your topic. I wouldn't waste my time with any directory that guarantees inclusion. The key is that the directory will check out your site and make sure it's legit before approving you. This is how you know it's a good directory. You may not get a lot of traffic, but getting in a few good directories is still an excellent step forward. A few of the more valuable ones to get you started:

- Dir.Yahoo.com
- BOTW.org
- DMOZ.org
- Blogged.com
- JoeAnt.com
- Greenstalk.com
- Familyfriendlysites.com

Forum commenting

Becoming involved in forums or message boards related to your topic and having a link to your blog in the signature line can send a few visitors your way. Google "your topic" and "forums," and you're sure to find a few. Just don't be annoying and go in just to promote yourself. People can see that from a mile away. The new age of the Internet is very much a "give and you shall receive" environment. If you seek to give and be a benefit before seeking your own rewards, you'll be much better off.

Linking to other blogs

I don't know what it is, but everyone wants to know when someone is talking about them. Bloggers are no different. When people link to my site, I get a notification and often go check out who linked to me and what the context was. I formed some positive relationships just from this. This is a great way to get on the radar of some small to medium-sized bloggers in your niche.

Create small topical pages

Squidoo.com, InfoBarrel.com, Hubpages.com, and a handful of others are sites that allow you to build a simple page about a topic. You can do it very quickly, and the pages often rank well in the search engines. If you build a page that gets a little bit of traffic and have links coming back to your site, you can catch some of those visitors. As if that weren't good enough, many of them allow you to earn money from your articles as well.

9. SEO tips for blogs

It takes a while to get a decent amount of traffic from the search engines. Generally, the search engines do not like NEW websites. They like more established sites that have a lot of people linking to them, proving they're reputable. This is why getting links from other bloggers, directories, other websites that have good reputations in the search engines' eyes is very important.

As your blog begins to grow by having more pages and more links, the search engines begin to send you more and more traffic. This is a good thing! But they're often wary of new websites, so time is your ally when it comes to the search engines.

SEO

Search Engine Optimization (SEO) is a science/art (depending on who you ask) that focuses on getting your website or blog to the top of the search engine listings. Being at the top of Google's results for any decent keywords can be a great source of traffic and the greatest part about it is that it's FREE TRAFFIC!

I won't get deep into SEO here. There are far more thorough books about it (for instance,

SEOBook.com), but as your blog grows, try to learn more about it because it will only help you. Just like most of the things you'll learn while blogging, you don't need to be an expert at it – just having a working knowledge will provide great results.

The thing to remember about the search engines (especially Google) is that they're trying to create a perfect system where any searchers can find exactly what they want. Google wants to display the most relevant websites. It will never have a perfect system, but it probably won't stop trying. If you can keep this in mind, it helps when you're trying to optimize your blog.

Don't waste your time trying to trick the search engines, they will figure it out and punish you for it. Just focus on making it very clear what your site is all about and writing worthwhile content for your reader, and the rest will take care of itself.

So, let's get to some SEO. **These are some of the most important pieces of SEO that every beginner should know.** If you do these right, you're that much ahead of most people who don't know anything about SEO.

1. Title tags

This may be the single most important part of on-page SEO. The title tag of your website is what shows up in the top of the browser window. It is also one of the most important factors the search engines use to determine what your site is about.

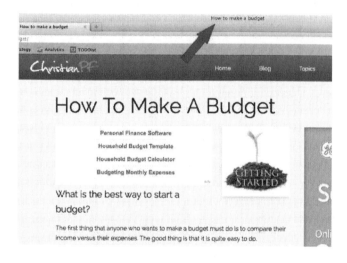

In the above picture you can see that the title tag is "How To Make A Budget" You WILL want to make sure that your title tags contain the keywords that you want to rank high enough in the search engines. If your site is about rock climbing, you will not want to have "welcome to Bill's blog" in the title tags. Something better would be "Rock climbing 101 | the best rock climbing techniques."

2. Anchor text

Anchor text – the text that people use when linking. For instance, if I created a link for a <u>great search engine</u>, you can see the link goes to Google. "Great search engine" is the anchor text. The anchor text is a big deal, because it tells the search engines what other sites say your site is about.

Google pays attention to what words are in the anchor text. Obviously, you can't control how other people link to your site all of the time. But, for those times that you can, use variations of your keywords when possible. Linking to other pages and posts on your website, directory submissions, blog carnivals and your signature line in forums all may be good places to make sure you can work your keywords into your anchor text.

3. Keyword research

If you're trying to get traffic from search engines, it's always a good idea to know what people are searching for before you start writing. I often use Aaron Wall's keyword tool and run some keyword ideas through it to get estimates of how many people are searching for them.

4. Get links

You already know the importance of links coming into your blog. <u>Getting links to your blog is still the single most important factor in getting traffic from the search engines.</u> Other than the great benefit they play in improving your search rankings, they also send visitors to your site. It's an obvious benefit but often overlooked by people focusing on SEO. If you get a link from a blog that gets a lot of visitors, you could see a huge traffic spike.

If you get links from lots of blogs, you can and will see visitors coming from most of them. Maybe not a bunch, but as you get more links, you will see more visitors. The bottom line about link-building is that you have to create something great that people want to link to. If you can consistently do that, many other things will fall into place.

Think about the whole process as building a house one brick at a time. And get excited each time you add a brick because it's slowly growing into the structure, and that brick is most likely going to remain there for years to come.

10. How I increased Adsense earnings $1500 in less than three months

This section is going to be a little bit beyond the basics, but these details can dramatically improve earnings from Adsense. Just to clarify, as I did this, I was already making some money with Adsense and had a pretty well established blog, but I had no idea how much difference a few tweaks could make.

In my case I increased earnings more than $1500 in a short amount of time. The thing you have to understand about Adsense is that no two sites are alike. Every blog has a different audience and different articles and most likely a different layout. All these things affect Adsense earnings. Knowing that, testing and trying new things is critical to find the winners!

1. Add a privacy policy

This is such a simple thing to do. I never realized that it's a "requirement" for Adsense publishers, but when I added a link in my footer to my Privacy Policy, there was a noticeable increase in earnings. I assume that Google rewards those who have a privacy policy and punishes those who don't by trimming their earnings. In a perfect world you want your lawyer to draft your privacy policy, but you're welcome to use mine for inspiration to make your life a bit easier (use at your own risk).

Find it here: http://seedtime.com/privacy-policy/

2. Put ads where people's eyeballs go

For me there's an eternal struggle between usability and profitability with ads. While I want/need to make money to pay my bills, I still want to make my blogs as user-friendly as possible. So, I made some sacrifices with some of them in order to maintain certain levels of usability, but one of the most important keys to making money with Adsense is ad placement.

As I mentioned before, you need to experiment with it. But for the first year or more I just kind of threw the ads wherever I had extra room. <u>Once I changed the location of my ads, my earnings tripled overnight.</u> It really freaked me out. I had no idea that just moving an ad a couple of inches would have such a dramatic effect.

3. Section targeting

This was another tweak I made that showed a noticeable difference in earnings. Basically, "section targeting" is telling Google what text on your site to look at when deciding what ads to show. Google is pretty good at figuring this out if you don't do this, but if you have a lot of stuff going on in your sidebars and footer sections, it's probably worth experimenting with. It's very easy to implement. You only need to use this tag

```
<!-- google_ad_section_start -->
```

to tell Google to start, and this tag

```
<!-- google_ad_section_end -->
```

to tell it to stop. I just added a text widget at the top of my post for the start tag and after the content for the end tag.

4. Quick Adsense plugin

This is a great WordPress plugin that allows you to put Adsense units within the body of your article. There are lots of criteria that you can select to really customize your ad placements.

43

Quick Tip: *Here's a piece of advice worth thousands of dollars to some of you. I've blogged for more than six years and have had Adsense on more than 10 blogs, and <u>I can tell you that almost without fail the most profitable spot to put an Adsense ad is directly below the article title on your blog post.</u> This plugin makes that very easy. So if you've never tried that location, go ahead and try it —you can thank me later.*

5. Change the colors

When Adsense first came out, people said to make the colors as loud and ugly as possible to draw attention to them. Next, I heard that the best thing to do was to blend them into the site. Of the two methods I think that blending works a little better and definitely looks a lot better!

I have a slight variation that works even better for me. Currently, I have most of my links set to a light blue color, not the usual blue. I used to have many of my Adsense ads match that, but I saw a nice increase when I changed the ad titles to the old standard Link Blue (aka #0000FF). I feel that visually it's a complement rather than a match. It stands out a little bit more but doesn't look bad either.

6. Write articles people are searching for

This might seem unrelated, but it's very important. If you're like most bloggers, you have a regular readership and you have readers from the search engines. For some reason a lot of bloggers just don't give much respect to search engine readers and don't really try to reach out to them other than trying to "convert" them to a regular reader.

I approach things a little bit differently. Rather than getting frustrated that so many search engine visitors don't come back, I started to embrace it. I realized that my main goal was to help people, so why should I care if they visit only once or on a daily basis as long as they're getting helped?

So while I very much appreciate and value my regular readers, I also understand that I can help those who find the site via a search engine. I started doing keyword research to see what people were looking for in the search engines. If there are people searching to find out how to start a budget, I want to help them find out!

What happened for me as I started to become more conscious of what people were searching for was that I started getting more search engine traffic – which, of course, leads to higher earnings from Adsense.

7. Add a Google search bar

This is a no-brainer. Google is the master of search, so you can bet that its search capability on your site is better than the default WordPress search tool. By installing this, you'll help your visitors find the information they're looking for on your site and make some extra cash in the process. When the search results (from the websites you choose) are displayed, they have the standard Google ads present, just like normal Google search results.

8. Link Google Analytics to Adsense

A while back, Google Analytics started to allow the option to integrate your Adsense data. This has helped me so much. It provides webmasters with a wealth of information about earnings. It's simple to see which articles are making the most money, which keywords are yielding the most, what sites send the most valuable traffic, and a whole lot more. If you use Adsense, don't pass this one up.

9. Test, retest and test again

When running Adsense tests, I typically let them run for a month in order to make sure they're very thorough. I have a calendar I use to mark down when I make changes and what changes I make. Then, when the test is complete, I compare CPM and eCPM (effective cost per thousand) rates to see what performed better. A/B split testing is a better method when possible, but for certain tests it just isn't possible or practical. Either way, if you want to make more money with Adsense, experimenting and testing is a must!

11. Seven tools that have helped make it all possible

Not all of these tools directly contribute to the bottom line, but each one of them proved very helpful over the last couple of years.

1. **Google Analytics** (google.com/analytics) – This is a wonderful (and free) statistics tool that will help you keep track of your visitors and analyze a lot of data about them. As I mentioned before, it now integrates with Adsense to give even more valuable data.

2. **Google Webmaster Tools** (google.com/webmasters/tools) – This will help you see how Google views your blog. It will also let you know whether there are any problems with it that you may not know about. I had some issues that were really hurting my search rankings, but I found out about them and fixed them and voila! All better.

3. **MailChimp Email Marketing Service** (mailchimp.com) – If you haven't started an email list for your blog, you definitely should consider it. Mailchimp makes it easy because the site offers this for free (up to 2000 subscribers) while no one else does this for free.

4. **SEObook Keyword Tool** (tools.seobook.com/keyword-tools) – I use

this to get a ballpark estimate of how many people are searching for particular keyword phrases.

5. **Hittail.com** – This one provides ideas for articles based on what you previously wrote about and could probably rank for. If you have a blog that's established, it might be worth paying $10 a month for it. Try using the free trial and see how much it helps you.

6. **Stock.xchng** – The best free stock photography site I have found.

7. **BigStock.com** - The best cheap stock photography site I have found. They have lots of images you can get for just about a buck.

A few more resources

- **My online blogging courses** – to dive deeper on this whole blogging thing, feel free to stop by EfficientBlogging.com to check out some of my blogging courses to help you start rocking it with your blog!

- **Scribe SEO tool for WordPress** –I tried it out and decided not to continue to use it because I thought it was priced a little too high for what I got from it. It can make the SEO process a bit easier, but I just wasn't sure about spending $27 on it. If the price comes down, I might recommend it a bit more.

12. Warnings for those starting out

Don't quit your day job

Even if you know a lot about making money with a blog (just by reading this book, you have a tremendous advantage over me when I started), it's going to take a while. This is not a get-rich-quick scheme, it's more of a work-for-free-for-a-long-time-and-then-reap-your-reward type of plan.

The beautiful thing is that I can now say it works if you're diligent and open to learning from your mistakes. But either way, conventional wisdom says, build your blog part-time and when you start making more from it than your day job, consider making it a full-time deal. My situation is a unique one, and I don't recommend doing what I did. In my case I am now thankful I got laid off. If I hadn't, I would probably still work at a job I didn't like!

Learn everything you can

One of the advantages I have is that I love to learn and don't stop when I make a mistake. I work really hard to learn from my mistakes and figure out what the better course of action is for the next time. You're going to do things wrong, but you just have to keep going and keep learning. Learning how to use Google search is very important. If you do, you can find an answer to just about every problem you encounter on the Web.

Avoid time-wasters

Checking your stats every hour, reading 500 blogs in your RSS, playing on Facebook, Twitter, Pinterest or Youtube all day will kill your productivity. Focus on what yields results and stay disciplined to stick with that. Social media is an important part of building traffic, but you have to keep it in check.

Have fun

While I wrote this book as a guide to help those who want to make money with a blog, I understand that many people don't really care about that. Either way, life is too short not to enjoy it. So, whether you want to be a full-time blogger or just communicate with friends – have fun!

Ready for more?

If you enjoy this book, for a limited time I am hosting a free 60-minute online workshop where I share the 3 biggest secrets that helped me turn my blog into a full-time living.

I will only be hosting these workshops for a limited time, so if you are interested be sure to pop over to get registered.

Just visit <u>EfficientBlogging.com/join</u> to get registered for free.

Thanks for reading!

I appreciate your feedback; it will help me continue to tweak and improve the book– so thank you in advance!

I wish you all the best on your blogging journey!

Sincerely,
Bob

Notes

Made in the USA
San Bernardino, CA
22 March 2017